Taking Car

by Elizabeth Moore

Consultant:
Adria F. Klein, Ph.D.
California State University, San Bernardino

capstone
classroom

Heinemann Raintree • Red Brick Learning
division of Capstone

Emma is taking care of her pet.

Jacob is taking care of his pet.

Emily is taking care of her pet.

Josh is taking care of his pet.

Madison is taking care of her pet.

Ben is taking care of his pet.

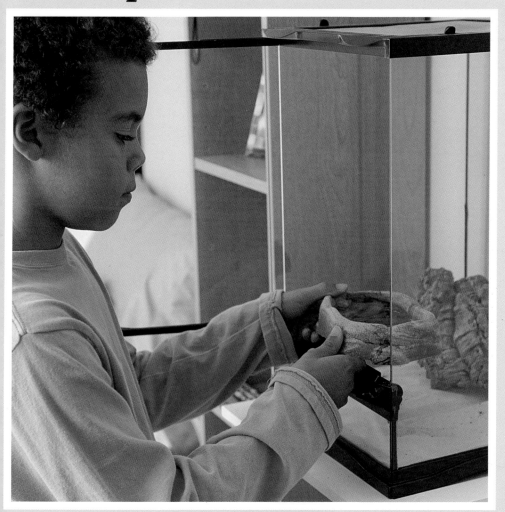

How do you take care of your pet?